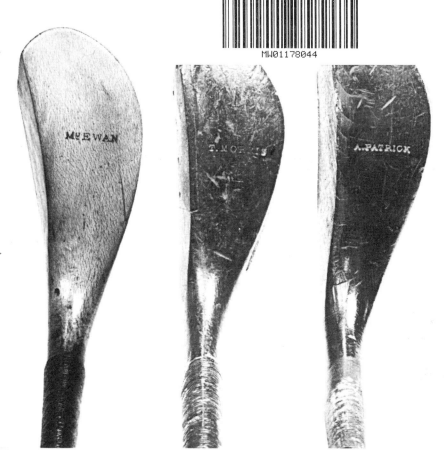

Three early long-nosed woods of about 1870. (Left to right) A McEwen mid spoon, a Tom Morris long spoon and another mid spoon by Alexander Patrick.

GOLFING BYGONES

Dale Concannon

Shire Publications Ltd

CONTENTS

Early golf 3

Golf clubs 7

Golf balls 15

Golf collecting 21

Further reading 32

Places to visit 32

Printed in Great Britain by C. I. Thomas & Sons (Haverfordwest) Ltd, Press Buildings, Merlins Bridge, Haverfordwest, Dyfed SA61 1XF.

British Library Cataloguing in Publication Data: Concannon, Dale. *Golfing Bygones.* 1. Golf. I. Title. 796. 352. ISBN 0-7478-0035-9.

To Austin and Tilda Concannon.

ACKNOWLEDGEMENTS
The author is grateful to the auction houses of Phillips, Sotheby's and Christies, whose help in providing the majority of photographs is much appreciated. I would especially like to thank Caroline Murdoch of Christies, Angus Gull and Bob Gowland of Phillips, and the press office staff at Sotheby's. Thanks, also, to innumerable private collectors for their help, especially to Bill Brett of Warwick, Walter Mechelli of Moseley Golf Club, Andy Gauld of Ratikoweg, West Germany, and Sarah Baddiel of Grays Gallery, London.

Cover: *Detail from 'The Bunker' by Charles Edmund Brock; dated 1894, oil on board. (Courtesy of Sotheby's.)*

'Musselburgh Links from the East', an oil painting by Robert Gemmell Hutchinson (1880-1936).

'A Dutch Golfing Scene', artist unknown. Before 1400 a version of golf called 'spel metten kolven' was played across open countryside or over the frozen Dutch lakes. This early sport has been suggested as the possible starting point for golf.

EARLY GOLF

The exact origins of golf are not known. Many theories have been put forward but none offers conclusive evidence as to where golf was first played or who played it: the date when a specific object was hit to a particular target and the number of 'hits' counted in between is open to question.

Throughout history various 'stick and ball' games have been played which bear a fleeting similarity to golf. As early as Roman times a sport called 'paganica' was popular. This involved striking a leather ball across open countryside but it is not known whether this was to any one target or even what clubs were used. Another game, called *jeu de mail*, or pall-mall as it became known in England, has also been discussed as a possible starting point for golf. Introduced into England from France in the early seventeenth century, it originally involved a ball being played 'croquet' style through a series of metal hoops. Played on a prepared surface with fixed boundaries, the aim of the game was to loft the ball through these hoops by means of a mallet not unlike an early golf club. *Jeu de mail*

suffered a loss of popularity in the early eighteenth century but not before it had developed into a game that was played out in the open.

Jeu de mail à la chicane, as it came to be known, developed from a sport played mainly on garden lawns into one played along tree-lined roads. Hitting to a target like a well or tree stump, the 'club' used was wooden with a lofted striking face. The ball, usually made of boxwood, was hit with a sweeping action comparable to a golf swing of the early nineteenth century. As in golf, the number of 'hits' was counted and the player who took fewest strokes emerged the victor. In a description of *jeu de mail* taken from *Historical Gossip about Golf and Golfers* (1863) the pastime was described thus: 'The goals (holes) are not very long, averaging perhaps half a mile. At the end of each is placed a touchstone, as it is called, which the players have to strike before the match is won, and he who can do it in the least number of strokes wins.'

While it is certain that *jeu de mail* and golf have striking similarities, it is generally thought that golf, in its earliest form, was probably already being played in Scotland and Holland many years before *jeu de mail* even came to England. However, it is also thought that *jeu de mail* certainly influenced the beginnings of golf around the London area. To this day Pall Mall takes its name from one of London's first 'courses', as does The Mall leading up to Buckingham Palace.

Nevertheless, informed opinion tends to favour either the Dutch or Scottish theories. The Dutch theory gained recognition as late as 1972 when the golf historian Steven Van Hengel published his book *Early Golf*. The basis of his work was that golf originated in Holland as early as the thirteenth century — some 150 years before the game was supposedly played in Scotland. Through exhaustive research into ancient Dutch archives, he proved that as early as 1296 there existed a short four-hole course at Loenen, a small town to the west of Utrecht. Using this as a starting point, Van Hengel traced the development of Dutch 'golf' over the next three hundred years.

Golf, he believed, came from the ancient Dutch game of *spel metten kolven* — a pastime later to be called *het kolven* or *kolf*. First played in the streets and churchyards of the older Dutch towns, the clubs and balls used were not unlike those used three hundred years later in Scotland. Gaining in favour, the game then moved into the countryside before eventually being played over designated courses, some time in the early fourteenth century, and played in winter over the frozen lakes of the Dutch lowlands.

Van Hengel offers a strong argument that *spel metten kolven* was indeed an early form of golf. Illustrating his book with the paintings of notable sixteenth-century Dutch artists, he demonstrated that holes were cut into the ice so that play was made possible. These paintings of everyday Dutch life show the identical nature of golf and this ancient pastime.

Van Hengel also surmised that golf was brought over to Scotland by fourteenth-century Dutch merchants on trading expeditions to the busy ports of Edinburgh and Leith. Because they often had to wait there, sometimes for months on end, he thought it more than likely that merchants not wishing to neglect their favourite pastime would bring their 'clubs' with them. Consequently, this theory does have some merit. The Scottish traditionalists who believe that Scotland is indeed the 'home of golf' completely dismiss this idea, however. They say that, while there is no doubt that there was a great deal of trade between Edinburgh and The Hague, it is open to question whether golf came from Holland to Scotland or the other way round.

The belief that Scotland was the birthplace of golf has proved difficult to back up with facts and figures. The Scottish archives have been far less illuminating than the ancient Dutch records which Van Hengel translated. The first reference to 'golfe' appears in an Act of James II in 1457. This statute expressed great concern that the king's army was neglecting archery practice in favour of playing golf and football. No other written references to golf can be found before this period but it is a fair assumption that golf, to reach this level of popularity, must have been played some years before.

This reference is the basis of the Scottish golf theory which maintains that golf has been played on the links land of Scotland for some six hundred years and dismisses the idea that a similar pastime played on ice had any influence on it whatsoever. According to this, 'true' golf did not develop from *spel metten kolven* or *kolf* but originated and flourished long before Dutch traders came across to Scotland.

Although there is no proof, it is generally thought that the very links land that golf was played over may offer a satisfactory answer to where the game began. Links land was originally a coastal area submerged by the incoming tide. As the silt and sand brought in by the sea built up, the shoreline gradually expanded, pushing back the area covered by water. This area of land newly reclaimed from the sea took its name from its geographical location, an area 'linking' the land to the sea, hence links land. Over a period of many hundreds of years grass began to grow on top of what was previously only silt and sand. This grass, unlike that found further inland, just covered the surface and never grew to any great

Left: *An early nineteenth-century English painting entitled 'William Gladstone as a Boy', artist unknown.*

Right: *A coloured mezzotint of John Taylor by Walter Cox after the original painting by Sir John Gordon Watson. Many famous amateur golfers were honoured in the nineteenth century by a portrait.*

length. It has been surmised that this aspect of links land, coupled with its natural contours, made it an ideal area for the first 'golfers'.

Golf, then, might have developed from the natural urge to strike pebbles and other objects along these grassed sand dunes, eventually giving way to a basic form of golf which involved club and ball. Like Van Hengel's Dutch theory, this idea has its merits but, until new information comes to light, both explanations of the possible origins of golf must remain only theories.

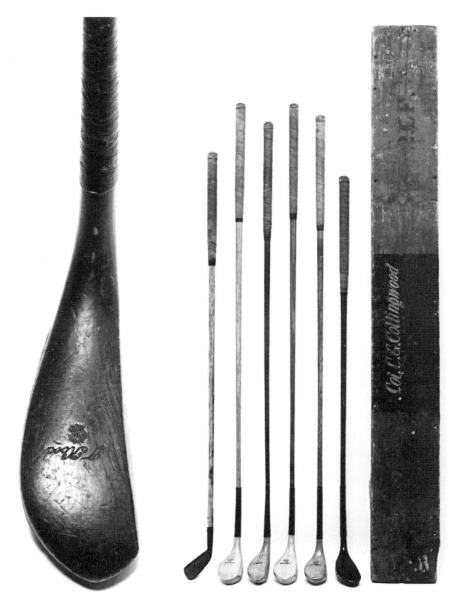

Left: *A Tom Hood long-nosed spoon made in Musselburgh about 1870.*

Right: *A most unusual set of scared head woods (about 1890), all stamped R. Forgan. These clubs, with one early iron, were found in their original transportation case and wrapped in 'The Times' newspaper.*

A selection of long-nosed clubs by master club-maker John Jackson of Perth, about 1830, and two blacksmith-made irons, about 1820.

GOLF CLUBS

The earliest written reference to club-making came in 1603 when it was official-ly noted that William Mayne had been appointed royal club-maker for life to the court of King James VI of Scotland. Unfortunately, no clubs made by William Mayne or any of his contemporaries have survived but the style in which they were fashioned is generally thought to have lasted well into the late nineteenth cen-tury.

From the early fourteenth century, and coinciding with the use of the feather ball, golf clubs were invariably made of wood (usually pear or thorn) and had a long, slender, 'pear-shaped' appearance. Known as 'long-nosed', this style was used from the earliest times until about 1850 and the advent of the harder gutta-percha ball.

Designed with the feather ball in mind, the head of the long-nosed wood had a slightly 'hooked' striking face and was normally about 5 inches (12.5 cm) in length from heel to toe. The back of the head had a small groove cut out to allow the insertion of lead for extra weight.

Also, for protection, a piece of ram's horn was cut into the base of the club to stop any possible splintering when used. The head was attached to a wooden shaft by means of a long-angled joint called a 'splice' or 'scar' (pronounced scare). The shaft and head were then bonded together with an animal-fat glue and sealed with pitched thread. The shaft, usually made of hickory, varied in overall length between 40 and 45 inches (1.02 to 1.14 metres). The grip would invariably have been made of leather. Bound top and bottom with a small binding of twine, it was usually about 5 inches (12.5 cm) in length. The colour of the head would vary considerably between golden beech brown, deep brown and almost black, depending on the wood used and the amount of beeswax polish used in the finishing.

On the top of the head would usually be stamped the club-maker's name or mark. From this we are able to gain a great deal of information about the club's age, its place of origin and the quality of workmanship. For example, if a long-

7

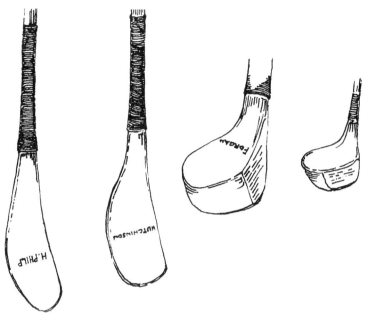

This illustration shows the change in wooden club heads from the long-nosed wood on the left (about 1830) through the transitional head to the bulger-headed woods of the early twentieth century. This development closely followed the change from the feather ball to the much harder gutta-percha ball of the mid to late nineteenth century.

nosed wood were marked 'H. Philp' we could assume that it was the work of Hugh Philp, master club-maker to the Society of St Andrews. Born in 1782, he was appointed to the post in 1819 and completed most of his best work after this period. Consequently it is likely that a Philp long-nosed wood would date from after 1819. It is also known that Hugh Philp was acknowledged in his own time as a club-maker of great skill who used only the best materials available. On the rare occasions that Philp clubs become available for sale they are generally considered desirable items of the highest quality.

Other highly regarded makes of long-nosed woods include those with the names of Cossar (1785-1811), W. and J. Dunn (1840-71), Jackson (1805-78), T. Morris (1821-1908) and A. Munro (1796-1847) as well as those stamped McEwen and Forgan — both prolific club-making families based at St Andrews. Clubs such as these are worth a great deal of money, but the collecting of 'long-noses' goes

beyond any financial consideration. They are accepted by the true collector as works of great beauty and are cherished as reminders of an age of craftsmanship.

THE EARLY IRONS

Until about 1820, a golfer's set was made up almost exclusively of long-nosed woods. However, as feather balls became increasingly expensive, the risk of damaging one by playing out of a carriage track, for example, became too great.

As a solution to this problem the first iron-headed clubs were made. These 'track' or 'rut' irons, as they came to be known, were usually custom-made by a local blacksmith. They were sturdy clubs with heavy heads, concave faces and a long, thick hosel (the neck of the club between the base of the shaft and the top of the head). After a time, golfers began to recognise the benefits of iron-headed clubs for general play and within a few years other utility irons began to evolve, such as the 'lofting iron' and the 'sand iron'.

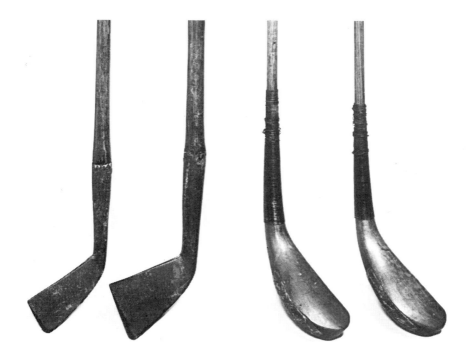

Above: *These extremely rare clubs are fine examples of late eighteenth-century workmanship. The irons were hand-forged with slightly hooked faces and heavily marked hosels. The woods are probably made of holly and are both unstamped.*

Below: *A couple of rare rut irons dating back to the early nineteenth century.*

The most renowned iron-makers of this early period were the Carrick family of Musselburgh (about 1830) and John Gray of Prestwick (about 1850). The work of these early craftsmen is now sought after.

With the gradual development of iron-headed clubs and, more importantly, the advent of the gutta-percha ball (in 1848), the era of the long-nosed woods was coming to an end.

THE TRANSITIONAL PERIOD

This was the period of change in golf club design, from about 1850 to 1890. It coincided with the demise of the feathery ball and the development of the more resilient gutta-percha ball. Quite simply, the old-style long-nosed woods were not strong enough to cope with the hardness of the first gutta balls: their long, slender heads had been designed for the feather ball and it was soon apparent that they had to change.

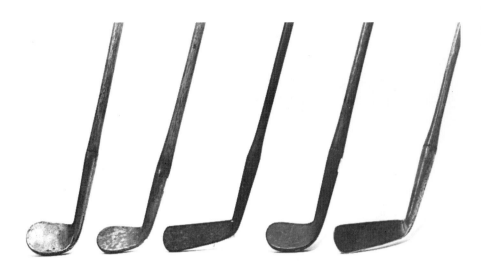

A selection of early nineteenth-century irons.

Some early iron-headed clubs, about 1865.

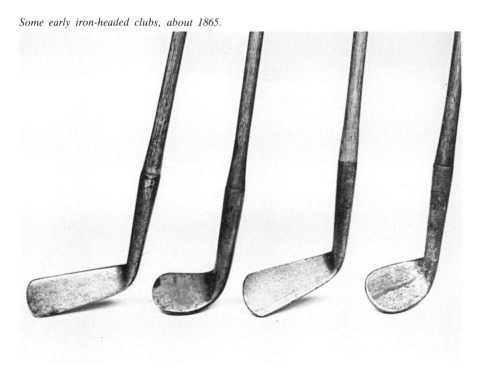

10

Above left: *(Left to right) A Paxton long-nosed grassed driver, a Philp long-nosed putter in fruitwood and another Philp putter made in the more common apple wood.*

Above right: *A long-nosed play club by Robert Forgan (left) and two by Tom Morris of St Andrews, about 1880.*

Below: *A selection of early aluminium putters.*

GARRICK

W.PARK
MAKER
MUSSELBURGH

JN.GRAY

GIBSON OF KINGHORN

ANDERSON

A.G.SPALDING
&BROS.

STEWART
OF ST.ANDREWS

R.FORGAN & SON
ST.ANDREWS

A.FORGAN
GLASGOW

M^CEWAN

J.B.HALLEY & CO.LTD

T.STEWART

A selection of club-makers' cleek marks. These marks were normally stamped on the backs of iron-headed clubs. Styles varied from a simple imprint of the maker's name to elaborate crests.

During this transitional period, iron-headed clubs became more extensively used and, eventually, wood-makers accepted that the only type of head that would stand the rigours of the gutta ball was one that was no more than half the length of an original long-nose.

WOODEN-SHAFTED CLUBS FROM 1890

After the transitional era, the only significant change in the design of wooden clubs was from a spliced head to that of a socket head joint (the shaft inserted into a hole in the head). This revolutionary change allowed wooden-headed clubs to be produced more cheaply, enabling many more people to play golf than ever before.

Golf began to be played much more widely and soon there were many more club manufacturers in England and Scotland. In the early twentieth century, woods and irons began to be mass-produced in response to this popularity and for the first time markings were put into the striking faces of iron-headed clubs. Following the traditions of the past, club-makers designed their own company motifs (called cleek marks) and stamped them on the backs of their irons as identification.

12

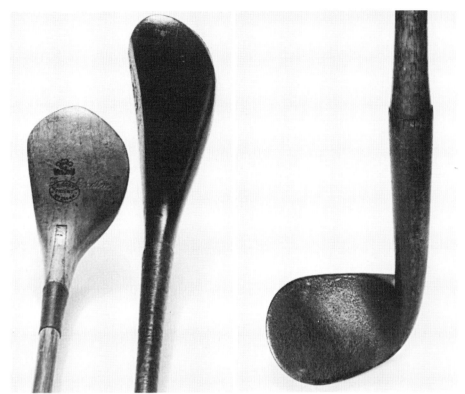

Above left: *This shows clearly the change in shape between the long-nosed club on the right and the mortice joint club of the early twentieth century.*

Above right: *An early track or rut iron of 1830 designed to extract the feathery from difficult lies such as those produced by old carriage tracks. It was designed with a concave face and a strong sturdy hosel.*

For the collector, this period offers a great deal of variety as well as the occasional bargain. From about 1900 onwards hundreds of patents were filed, dealing with weird and wonderful inventions like 'spring-faced irons', 'Urquhart adjustables', 'Mills' aluminium clubs' and many more.

The wooden-shafted hickory era lasted until about 1935 when the first steel shafts were introduced. Unusual and interesting clubs were patented during the first few years of the 'steel' era, but very few worthy of note. Perhaps in another two hundred years or so collectors might feel differently.

From about 1850 use of the long-nosed putter declined and in its place came the iron-headed club. The first generation of metal putters were of a simple blade design but from about 1880 onwards more elaborate putters became the fashion. Here is a small selection of the more unusual designs.

Various modern South African caddy clubs which are probably not unlike the early clubs used by the Scottish club carriers of the early nineteenth century.

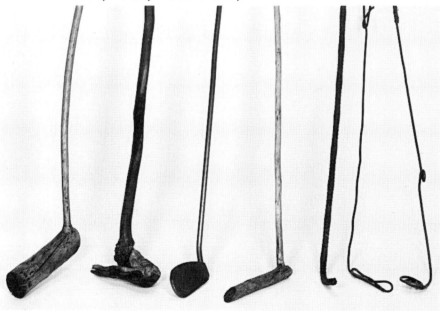

Some fine examples of Gourlay feather balls, about 1820. The numbers stamped on each ball denote size or weight.

GOLF BALLS

THE FEATHER BALL

From about the year 1400 until midway through the nineteenth century the feather ball was used for golf. The 'feathery', as it was more commonly known, took its name from the goose feathers used to fill what was originally three pieces of bull's hide stitched together with twine.

The goose feathers, supposedly a top hat full, were boiled and then mashed into a pulp. They were then put by hand into their leather receptacle — easily at first and then, as the ball took shape, with increasing force. A few final stitches closed the seam, sealing in the mixture, and it was rounded with one or two hammer blows.

Finally it would be left to dry, during which time the goose feathers expanded and the leather shrank, producing a hard ball of about the right size and weight: usually about 1.8 inches (4.6 cm) in diameter and between 0.85 and 1.06 ounces (24 and 30 grams) in weight.

Because it was made of leather, there were many drawbacks to the feather ball — not least its tendency to fall apart in the rain, a common hazard when playing golf in Scotland! They were also very expensive to buy: a top ball-maker might produce perhaps three or four balls a day and was not inclined to sell them cheaply.

In 1618 King James VI officially noted: 'No small quantitie of gold and silver is transported yearlie out of His Highness's kingdome of Scotland for the buying of goff balls.' His Majesty insisted on a 'Pryce of no more than four shillings money of this realme' when granting a golf-ball monopoly to James Melville and associates. This royal concern eventually led to the price of feathery balls being set at between 2s 6d and 3s 6d, depending on who made them.

Unfortunately no feathery balls of James Melville exist today but balls made by other master ball-makers have survived. Not least among these are those marked Gourlay — a famous ball-making family based for the most part at Musselburgh on the east coast of Scotland. 'Gourlay featheries' are highly prized and have an auction value which reflects this.

Left: *A feather golf ball marked Allan (Robertson) and with the owner's initials 'D.W.', about 1830.*
Right: *A feather ball by D. Marshall.*

Other rare and valuable feather balls include those marked with the name of Tom Morris (1821-1908), four times winner of the original British Open champion's belt and acknowledged as the 'Grand Old Man of Golf'. Another rare find might be a ball marked 'Allan', which would be the work of Allan Robertson, the first man ever to play around the Old Course at St Andrews in 79 strokes and possibly the game's first professional. Born in 1815, Robertson was the master ball-maker who taught Tom Morris how to make his first featheries. As both were relatively late feather ball-makers, examples of both Robertson's and Morris's work still survive in private collections as well as in the major golf museums. However, no work of the early ball-makers has yet come to light, although feather balls are known to have been made by William Dickson of Leith (about 1629), George Law of St Andrews (about 1770) and the Patterson brothers

Left: *An early hand-cut gutta-percha ball, about 1850.*
Right: *A late gutta ball made by the Park family, about 1884.*

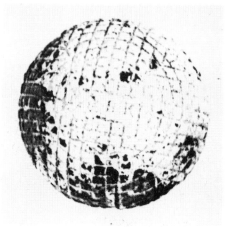

'Old' Tom Morris of St Andrews, a legendary figure in the history of golf, was renowned not only for his great playing ability but also for his ball-making skills. Morris was apprenticed to feather ball-maker Allan Robertson, where he first learned how to stitch bull's hide. He went on to become a famous feather ball-maker himself by the mid nineteenth century and was one of the first to experiment with the 'new' gutta-percha balls.

(about 1620) as well as James Melville of St Andrews (about 1615).

The art of the feather ball-maker survived for many hundreds of years and the skill of feather ball-making became a closely guarded secret. Despite this, its end came quickly and almost without warning in 1848 with the introduction of the first gutta-percha ball.

THE GUTTA-PERCHA BALL

Gutta-percha — a type of India-rubber solution — was supposedly introduced into England in the early nineteenth century. The story goes that it first came to London as packing around an Indian idol on its journey from the Far East. It was soon found to be an excellent material for making golf balls. Pliable when heated, it was easily shaped by hammer into a rough sphere. On hardening, it was further smoothed by hand, using a file, and then it was painted, normally white for general play or red for use in the snow.

It was not a success when first introduced in 1848 despite being far cheaper to produce than the feather ball. The biggest drawback initially was a highly erratic flight when struck. However, it was found almost by accident that after a period of use the gutta ball performed better when badly marked than it did when perfectly smooth. Eventually it became common practice for golfers to give their caddies two or three new balls to 'play in' until marked enough to hand back.

Around 1860, gutta ball-makers began, as common practice, to hand-cut each ball before use, realising the aerodynamic benefits of a marked ball, and a cold chisel was used to incise an overall mesh pattern which completely eliminated the hitherto erratic flight.

In 1875 hand-cut marking gave way to a new method which produced a more uniform mesh pattern. It was soon found that by placing the heated gutta-percha into a crude mould, it could be shaped far more efficiently than by hand. The inside of the mould was already lined with a mesh pattern which would indent the ball when the mould was closed. This moulded mesh pattern proved far superior to the old hand-cut markings and

quickly became the preferred method of golf-ball manufacture. This relatively simple innovation heralded a new era: golf balls became much cheaper to produce and therefore cheaper to buy. They were also far more available to the majority of golfers because, after a short time, manufacturers were able to mass-produce them in enough numbers to satisfy public demand.

In the last few years of the nineteenth century public demand grew ever stronger and spurred golf-ball manufacturers on to produce even more aerodynamically efficient designs. In 1885 a new pattern called the 'bramble' was introduced which covered the surface of the ball in a series of tiny pimples instead of meshed lines. This design proved popular with the golfing public and flourished even after the introduction of the rubber core ball in 1898.

The gutta-percha ball reigned supreme for over forty years, with colourful names like the 'Agrippa', the 'Woodley Flier', 'Paxton's Perfection' and the 'Silvertown', bringing golf into the modern age.

THE RUBBER-CORE BALL

In 1898 the first rubber-core golf ball appeared — so called because of the tightly wound rubber thread used in its construction. Essentially, the modern ball is the direct descendant of the first rubber-core balls of the early twentieth century. Unlike its predecessors, the feathery and the gutty, the new rubber-core aroused a great deal of controversy.

The first rubber-core ball was patented in 1898 in Akron, Ohio, by a wealthy entrepreneur, Coburn Haskell, in partnership with the B. F. Goodrich Company. The first patented ball was called the Haskell after its inventor. It proved moderately successful at the start, mainly because people were curious about it. The ball, however, had two main drawbacks: it was very expensive and it was very unpredictable in flight. Using the mesh-marked pattern of the old gutties, it had a tendency to dip in flight and soon picked up the sarcastic title of the 'Bouncing Billy'. This problem was solved in 1899 when Haskell changed the mesh pattern to a dimple-style bramble pattern — a style favoured by the last

A brass gutta-percha golf-ball mould by John White and Company, Edinburgh.

generation of gutties.

Confident of success, Haskell and the Goodrich Company extended their patent to cover Britain as well as the United States, and when Sandy Herd won the British Open at Hoylake in 1902 using a Haskell ball for all four rounds its success seemed assured. A licensing agreement was set up between Haskell and a number of British golf companies as early as 1900 but this agreement was soon broken. In 1905 Haskell sued the Hutchison, Main Company of Glasgow for breaking his patent by producing their own rubber-core balls. Nationalistic fervour gripped Scotland and the case was soon front-page news all over the world. The English court found that Haskell's patent was void on the ground that the concept was not original and therefore not binding. To add insult to injury, British golf companies then tried to export their own rubber-core balls to America, but fortunately for Haskell this was successfully blocked by the American courts.

Rubber-core balls dominated sales all over the world for many years, during which there were many alterations and improvements to the design. In 1905 a major innovation was patented by an

(Left to right) A Spalding 27½, a late mesh-marked gutty, a painted gutty, a silver-plated bramble-patterned rubber core and a William Gourlay feathery.

Englishman, W. Taylor. His design for a dimple-patterned ball was to prove revolutionary as it was the forerunner to the golf ball we use today. Unfortunately for Taylor it was too radical for the time and was not incorporated in golf-ball design for another twenty years. One innovation that did receive widespread acclaim was Eleazer Kempsall's patent for a liquid core in 1910. This involved a pressurised central rubber core which considerably aided the flight of the golf ball and the design remained in use for a long time.

In the mid 1920s the golfing authorities of both Britain and America decided to standardise the overall weight and size of the ball. This inevitably ended the era of the highly individual item: the golf ball has not changed significantly since. Millions of golf balls are manufactured annually but collectors search for rare items manufactured before 1920 when golf balls were uniform in neither size nor design.

Without doubt, the most sought-after ball produced after 1898 is the first mesh-marked Haskell. Not as rare as a feather ball or an early hand-cut gutta, Haskells were made for only a short time and are difficult to find.

The following is a brief chronology of the development of the golf ball.

Feather ball: used from the earliest days until the advent of the gutta-percha ball.

First gutta-percha ball: 1848-50.

First hand-cut gutta balls: 1850-75.

First moulded gutta balls: 1875-98.

Rubber-core balls: 1898 onwards (including the standardisation between 1925 and 1928 of the size and weight of golf balls).

THE

G O F F.

AN

Heroi - Comical Poem,

IN

THREE CANTOS.

++

Cetera, quæ vacuas tenuissent carmina mentes,
Omnia jam volgata.   VIRG.

++

The Second EDITION.

++

E D I N B U R G H:

Printed for JAMES REID, Bookseller in *Leith.*
M.DCC.LXIII.   (Price Four-pence)

'The Goff', an heroi-comical poem in three cantos by Thomas Mathison, is one of golf's rarest and most valuable treasures. This shows the front cover of the second edition published in 1763.

A selection of golfing books including Robert Clark's 'Golf. A Royal and Ancient Game' and Robert Forgan's 'Golfer's Handbook' (1890).

GOLF COLLECTING

Golf collections have been in existence in one form or another for the past three hundred years. As early as 1793, in a poem entitled 'The Goff', it was noted that one of the players in a particular match had accumulated hundreds of 'olde goff clubes'.

The next known written reference to a golf collection is one of 1866, when an advertisement appeared on the back cover of a golf magazine announcing the opening of a museum in the Union Club House at St Andrews. This museum was to be dedicated to the 'Old Relics of Golfing Celebrities and other objects of interest in connection with the game'. This collection, later thought to have been housed at the Royal and Ancient Golf Club, was apparently in recognition of the great public interest shown in golf's history and development.

By the end of the nineteenth century it

became quite fashionable to own a collection of 'golfing bygones'. Old clubs, books and feathery golf balls all made excellent conversation pieces at formal social gatherings. In 1901, at the International Exposition in Glasgow, many of these private collections were exhibited as well as the best pieces from the St Andrews museum.

As a result of this growth of interest, Harry B. Wood published *Golfing Curios and the Like* in 1910. This was the first publication to deal comprehensively with golfing memorabilia. A great golf collector himself, Wood donated his entire collection to the North Manchester Golf Club, where, unfortunately, it no longer exists.

Another publication dealing with a particular facet of golf collecting was Cecil Hopkinson's *Collecting Golf Books* (1938). A thorough study of golfing

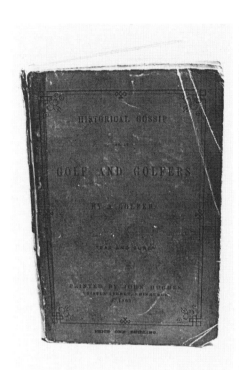

GOLFIANA;

OR,

NICETIES CONNECTED WITH THE

GAME OF GOLF.

DEDICATED, WITH RESPECT,

TO THE

MEMBERS OF ALL GOLFING CLUBS,

AND TO THOSE OF

ST. ANDREWS AND NORTH BERWICK

IN PARTICULAR.

BY GEORGE FULLERTON CARNEGIE.

EDINBURGH:
WILLIAM BLACKWOOD, 45, GEORGE STREET; AND
ALEXANDER HILL, 50, PRINCES' STREET.

1833.

Price 10/6.

Left: *The 1863 publication 'Historical Gossip about Golf and Golfers' by 'A Golfer' (G. Robb).*
Right: *An early and very rare book by George Fullerton Carnegie called 'Golfiana; or Niceties Connected with the Game of Golf', published in 1833.*

literature, it is now a highly sought-after book itself.

The next chapter in the development of 'golfiana' came in 1950 when a museum was established by the United States Golf Association in New York. This rapidly encouraged interest in America and within the next few years other major exhibitions were established all over the United States.

Since then there has been a steady growth in golf collecting all over the world, especially in Japan and West Germany. Sales of golfing memorabilia are now a common occurrence in auction houses everywhere and now, most significantly, a National Museum of Golfing Bygones is to be built on the Bruce Embankment at St Andrews in Scotland. Not unlike the old museum at St Andrews, this will be dedicated to golf's past and treasures that hitherto went abroad will now have a permanent resting place in 'The Home of Golf'.

GOLF BOOKS

The first written reference to golf occurred in 1457 when King James II of Scotland issued the proclamation that 'the Fut ball and Goff be utterly cryit dune'. It appears that both sports were interfering with the army's archery practice!

The most valuable golf publication ever to come to auction was 'an heroi-comical poem in three cantos' called *The Goff.* Dated 1743, its author was Thomas Mathison. Acknowledged as a great rarity, it fetched over £17,000 at a Phillips auction in 1985.

This poem, however, is not considered the rarest of all golfing titles; that distinction goes to a publication in 1721 by James Arbuckle called the *Glotta*. This is considered to be the first literary work on golf and, while its text has been reproduced in later publications, no copies of the original have ever come to auction. This short extract from the *Glotta*, explaining the meaning of golf, is from *Golfiana Miscellanea* by James Lindsey Stewart, published in 1887.

'The timber curve to leather orb apply,
These to the distant hole direct they drive,
They claim the stakes who thither first arrive.'

From about 1885 golf became very popular and many more books were printed to keep pace with public demand. Among the highly collectable golf books that were published during this time were *Golfiana Miscellanea* (1887) by James Lindsey Stewart, *The Game of Golf* (1896) by Willie Park, *The Golf Book of East Lothian* (1896) by the Reverend John Kerr, *Half Hours with an Old Golfer* (1895) by Calamo Currente and *Reminiscences of Golf on St Andrews Links* (1887) by James Balfour.

Golf book collecting is enjoyable as well as rewarding. Golfing literature offers an insight into the development of the game and how the authors felt about it — their hopes and desires for the future

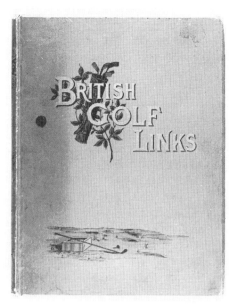

Above: 'British Golf Links' by Horace Hutchinson (1897) is illustrated with many fine early photographs of Britain's best known courses.

Below: 'The Golf Book of East Lothian' by the Reverend John Kerr. A highly informative book, it describes much of the early history of golf. Illustrated are two differents editions of the same book.

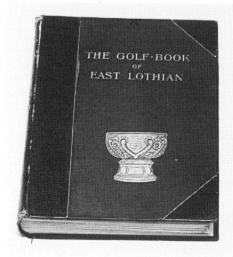
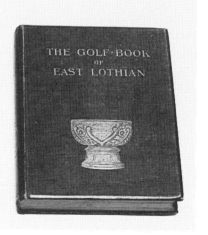

Two pen and ink sketches by Harry Furniss for the book 'The Haunted Major' by R. Marshall.

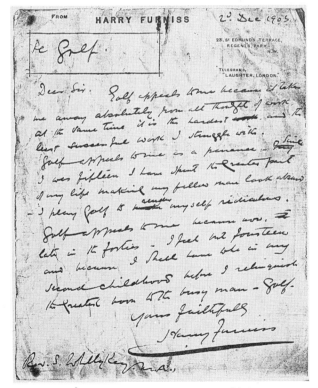

A letter written in 1903 by the artist Harry Furniss.

'Golf appeals to me because it takes me away absolutely from all thought of work. At the same time it is the hardest and least successful work I struggle with.

Golf appeals to me as a penance:— since I was fifteen I have spent the greater part of my life making my fellow man look absurd — I play golf to render myself ridiculous.

Golf appeals to me because now, late in the forties, I feel but fourteen and because I shall have to be in my second childhood before I relinquish the greatest boon to the busy man — golf.'

'Anon' by 'Shortspoon' (Major F. P. Hopkins). This fine watercolour clearly illustrates what golf must have been like in the early nineteenth century — golfers playing with long-nosed clubs, feather balls and dressed in the sensible suits of the period. The caddies are each carrying the clubs of their masters, who are teeing off just a few paces from where they had just putted out.

of golf as well as their comments on its past.

For the collector starting his own golf library, good advice would be to collect the titles of one particular author or authors. Bernard Darwin would be a good start. His books are valued from just a few pounds to many hundreds. Henry Cotton was also a prolific writer who had many titles published — again very good value as well as interesting to read.

GOLF ART

For the past two hundred years, golf has proved a popular subject for painters, etchers, engravers and sculptors. Most champion golfers and classic golf courses have been portrayed on canvas or in marble.

Lemuel Francis Abbott (1760-1803) is considered to have been one of the first painters of golfing scenes. The 'Blackheath Golfer', golf's earliest and most famous print, was a reproduction of Abbott's original painting of William Innes, Captain of Royal Blackheath.

The first prints were taken in 1790 by Valentine Green as a mezzotint engraving. Another engraving was taken of Abbott's second major work — a portrait of Henry Callender, also Captain of Blackheath. This print by William Ward, like the first by Valentine Green, holds great value as a collector's item and always proves popular when put through auction. Other notable artists of this early period include Sir George Chalmers (1720-91), David Allan (1744-96) and Sir John Gordon (1788-1864).

As the years went on, golfing prints became fashionable in club houses as well as private homes. In 1890 *Vanity Fair* magazine published a series of lithographic prints featuring prominent golfers of the age. However, all the 'prominent' golfers featured were 'gentlemen amateurs' and it was not until 1897 that a truly great player, Tom Morris of St Andrews, was even considered as a subject. In 1903 an oil painting of the 'Grand Old Man of Golf' was commissioned by the Royal and Ancient Golf Club of St Andrews as recognition not only of his skill as a player but of his many years of dedicated service as their greenkeeper.

This was to herald a new era for the professionals of the time. Players of the calibre of James Braid, Harry Vardon, Ted Ray and Abe Mitchell were all illustrated in turn — this at a time when they were not even allowed in the club house without the express permission of a member! As their fame increased, so did

Left: *A photogravure of Tom Morris of St Andrews.*

Right: *A humorous watercolour by Harry Rountree entitled 'Serious Bridger' (1920).*

the appreciation of the role of the professional. They became household names and their images were used, as today, for the promotion of golf equipment and other items. Some of golf's most interesting pieces of art come from these early advertisements.

The great golf courses soon became a source of inspiration for painters and etchers alike. Possibly the most famed artist in this field was Harry Rountree (1880-1950). Born in New Zealand, he is best known for the illustrations in Bernard Darwin's book *The Golf Courses of the British Isles* (1910). His work has always been highly valued.

After Rountree, there are hundreds of artists, etchers and engravers worthy of note. A few of the more collectable names include Sir Leslie Ward (1851-1922), famous for his 'Spy' caricatures, illustrator Frank Paton (1856-1909), George Pipeshank (about 1819), watercolour artist of the Cope's cigarette card series John Hassell (1868-1948), J. Temple (about 1890), Bernard Partridge (1861-1945) and the famous golfing sculptors Hal Ludlow (statue of Harry Vardon, 1899), William Tyler (Horace Hutchinson, 1890) and Alex Macleay (John Ball, 1893).

Despite the fact that a great deal of golfing art is in private hands, there still remains a considerable amount on public view in many places. Most major golf clubs, like Royal Troon, Sunningdale and Hoylake, have large collections of golfing art but the permission of the club must be sought before viewing.

Possibly the most collectable set of golfing cigarette cards is Cope's Golfers (1900).

CERAMICS

The golden era of golfing ceramics was between 1890 and 1939. As playing golf became more and more fashionable, so did the buying of golf-related pieces of porcelain and pottery.

Early pieces can be of great value, especially when hand-painted. The most popular names to collect are Royal Doulton, Wedgwood, Mackintyre Burslem, Copeland Spode and Minton.

The majority of designs with golfing motifs were made for practical items like water jugs and plates. As time went on these items became mass-produced, with Royal Doulton leading the way with their 'Perrier' style character design. These figures were slightly surrealistic and were commissioned by Perrier.

ADVERTISING FIGURES

From the early twentieth century, golf

A rare Royal Doulton ceramic jardiniere of about 1915.

27

(Left to right) A Royal Doulton Kingsware whisky flask, a brown glazed Royal Doulton jug, another Royal Doulton jug painted with golfing figures in the style of Bateman and a Royal Doulton Kingsware pottery jug.

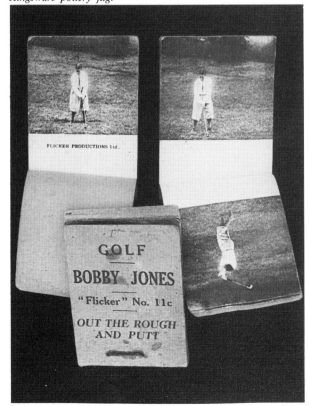

Three Bobby Jones 'Flicker' books of about 1930. They consist of a sequence of rapid film photographs which, when thumbed through, create the illusion of movement.

Above: *A silver-gilt Open Championship medal presented to Jack Simpson for winning the 1884 Golf Championship at Prestwick.*

Left: *A decorative golfing spirit flask of the early 1920s.*

Below: *A silver vesta case with an Edwardian golfing scene enclosed by two onyx ashtrays by Asprey, also with a golfing theme.*

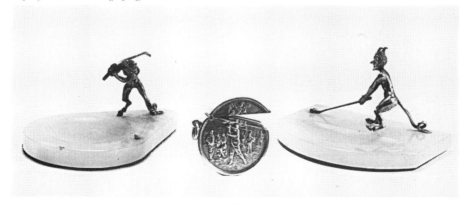

29

This golfing figure dressed in plus-fours was typical of the statues produced in the early twentieth century.

manufacturing companies began to realise the benefits of using pottery or plaster figures to promote their goods.

Both Dunlop and Penfold used plaster golfing figures to promote their golf balls. Golf professional shops were given these items to advertise the latest models. Designed as 'golfing caricatures', both the 'Dunlop Man' and the 'Penfold Man' were supposed to represent a typical golfer of the period: plus-fours, tweed jacket, shirt and tie.

Realising the benefits of such a promo-

tion, two other golf-ball manufacturers also decided to release their own golfing figures. The North British Rubber Company produced the 'Scottie Dog' around 1930 and the 'Silvertown Man' was introduced at the same time by the Silvertown Golf Company. Less common than either the Penfold or Dunlop figures, the 'Scottie Dog' took the form of a black Scottish terrier with a golf ball between its teeth. The 'Silvertown Man', not unlike the Dunlop figure, was a little golfing man with a golf ball for a head.

Unfortunately, being made of either plaster or papier-mâché, all these figures were easily broken and consequently they are not especially common today, although by no means rare. Many were also thrown away by golf professionals eager to promote the latest brand of golf ball in much the same way as old advertisements are discarded today. Despite this, these figures can still be seen in the occasional club professional's shop and are well worth a close examination. All these figures are still very collectable. Individually they fetch reasonable amounts at auction but a prize for any collector would be to own a complete set of four.

CIGARETTE CARDS

Since about 1890 golf has proved a popular subject for cigarette-card makers. Prominent golfers, famous courses and golf trophies have all been covered at one time or another.

The most collectable golfing cigarette cards are Churchman's Famous Golfers, Player's Championship Golf Courses, Marsuma's Famous Golfers and Their Strokes (1914) and Cope's Golfers (1900). For cartophilists (cigarette-card collectors) the rarest of those mentioned are the Cope's Golfers — and a complete set of fifty is especially valuable.

GOLF EPHEMERA

The collecting of golf-related ephemera is an absorbing pastime. As the term 'ephemera' implies, it covers a multitude of diverse and interesting items such as car mascots, advertisements, toys, programmes, scorecards, buttons, postcards, medals, autographs, early tee-pegs, stamps and a vast range of silver-

'The Links of St Andrews' by James Kinnear.

ware.

High on the list of desirable golfing ephemera are the Bobby Jones 'Flicker' books, a series of early black and white 'rapid film' photographs illustrating the classic swing of golf's greatest amateur.

For anyone interested in golfing bygones, ephemera offer not only an excellent starting point to any collection but give an invaluable insight into golf's history and development through the years.

Golfing bygones.

FURTHER READING

Cotton, Henry. *Golf: A Pictorial History*. Collins, 1975.
Darwin, Bernard. *A History of Golf in Britain*. Cassel, 1952.
Dobereiner, Peter. *The Glorious World of Golf*. McGraw Hill, New York, 1973.
Henderson, I. T., and Stirk, D. *Golf in the Making*. Henderson and Stirk, 1979.
Olman, Morton W. *The Encyclopaedia of Golf Collectables*. Books Americana, Alabama, 1985.
Taylor, John. *Golf Collectors' Price Guide*. St Giles, 1983.
Watt, Alick A. *Collecting Old Golfing Clubs*. A. A. Watt and Son, Alton, Hampshire, 1985.

PLACES TO VISIT

Intending visitors are advised to find out dates and times of opening before making a special journey. In addition to the places listed below, Sotheby's, Phillips and Christies auction houses are excellent places to visit on the viewing days before the major golfing sales.

GREAT BRITAIN

Gullane Golf Museum, Gullane Golf Club, Gullane, East Lothian, Scotland. Telephone: 087 57277. An excellent collection, the majority of which comes from Archie Baird, a respected golf historian.

North Berwick Museum, School Road, North Berwick, East Lothian, Scotland. Telephone: 0620 3470. Collection of clubs, balls and art relating to the North Berwick club.

Royal and Ancient Golf Club, St Andrews, Fife, Scotland. Telephone: 0334 72112. Very private, it offers the greatest collection of 'golfiana' in the world. Long-noses, feather balls, ceramics, silverware, art and literature are all extensively covered.

Spalding Collection, Dundee, Angus, Scotland. Telephone: 0382 645443. Small collection of clubs and memorabilia relating to this famous golf company.

Troon Golf Club, Troon, Ayrshire, Scotland. Telephone: 0292 311555. The 'Early Clubs' are housed at Royal Troon. Found some years ago in Hull, they are believed to date back to the late eighteenth century, making them the earliest known golf clubs anywhere.

UNITED STATES OF AMERICA

Museum and Library of the United States Golf Association, Far Hills, New Jersey. Possibly the largest collection of golfing literature anywhere in the world.

World Golf Hall of Fame, Pinehurst, North Carolina. Best collection of early long-nosed woods and general golfing bygones in the United States.